The Little Book

A Collection of Alternative 12 Steps

by Roger C.

Second Edition

AA Agnostica

The Little Book:
A Collection of Alternative 12 Steps

Second Edition

Published by AA Agnostica

ISBN 978-1-7774832-1-0

Every effort has been made to trace ownership of copyright materials; in the event of an inadvertent omission or error, please notify the publisher.

The information, ideas, and suggestions in this book are not intended as a substitute for professional advice. Before following any suggestion contained in this book, you should consult your personal physician or mental health professional. Neither the author nor the publisher shall be liable or responsible for any loss or damage allegedly arising as a consequence of the use or application of any information or suggestions in this book.

The Twelve Steps are reprinted in Part Three with permission from Alcoholics Anonymous World Services, Inc. ("AAWS") Permission to reprint these excerpts does not mean that AAWS has reviewed or approved the contents of this publication, or that AAWS necessarily agrees with the views expressed herein. AA is a program of recovery from alcoholism only – use of the Twelve Steps in connection with programs and activities which are patterned after AA, but which address other problems, or in any other non-AA context, does not imply otherwise.

Table of Contents

Acknowledgments

I want to thank the members and founders of secular AA groups. Over the last years they have been an invaluable source of support and inspiration.

Thank you, as well, to all those that put together alternative versions of the Steps. This work provides alcoholics with the liberty to go forward in recovery with 12 Steps and without having to adhere to any form of religious belief.

I am particularly grateful to Gabor Maté, Stephanie Covington, Allen Berger, and Thérèse Jacobs-Stewart for allowing their (secular) interpretations of each one of the 12 steps to be shared in this book.

Without the encouragement of William L. White and Ernest Kurtz, I would never have written *The Little Book*. Thanks to both of them.

A personal thank you to Karen and to my brother Ron.

Thanks to you all for helping me to better understand my life, one day at a time.

Foreword

"Here are the steps we took, which are suggested as a program of recovery."

(*Alcoholics Anonymous*, 1939, p. 71)

The worldwide growth of Alcoholics Anonymous (AA) and the adaptation of AA's Twelve Steps to innumerable problems of living stand as "living proof" of the catalytic power of this framework for personal transformation. The growth of secular, spiritual, and religious alternatives to AA also confirms AA co-founder Bill Wilson's 1944 declaration, "the roads to recovery are many" (Wilson, 1944/1988). In 2006, Ernest Kurtz, author of *Not-God: A History of Alcoholics Anonymous*, and I published an essay entitled "the varieties of ✳ recovery experience." In that essay, we contended that these growing "varieties" within and beyond AA constitute one of the most important milestones in the history of addiction recovery. Roger C. has provided a valuable service in illustrating such varieties through this collection of how AA's Twelve Steps have been adapted and interpreted across diverse philosophical, professional, religious, and cultural traditions.

While some grateful AA members perusing this book will think it heresy to change the wording of AA's Twelve Steps, others will recognize that such tolerance and even celebration of the varieties of recovery experience are deeply rooted with the historical culture of AA. Consider the following from AA co-founder Bill Wilson:

> *Alcoholics Anonymous does not demand that you believe in anything. All of its Twelve Steps are but suggestions.*
>
> *It is a tradition among us that the individual has the unlimited right to his own opinion on any subject under the sun. He is compelled to agree with no one; if he likes, he can disagree with everyone.*
>
> *AA's orthodoxy, if it can be called that, is merely what the majority experience suggests. You can still take your pick!*

The growing varieties of AA experience and secular and religious alternatives to AA are reflected in two emerging worldwide trends.

First, references to "Are you in the Program?" once referred to one's identification with a particular recovery fellowship. Answers to this question today are likely to reflect identification with a much broader 12-Step community. What is emerging is a more encompassing "12-Step cultural consciousness" that reflects an expanded definition of "recovery community" — one that embraces multiple "communities of recovery." How such consciousness will expand the doorways of entry into recovery and be mobilized as a force for cultural change remains to be seen.

Second, the philosophical diversification of recovery pathways and the recognition of the viability of alternative pathways are creating a larger level of mutual identification. People who once defined themselves only as AA, NA, SOS, SMART Recovery, WFS, or Celebrate Recovery members are today much more likely to also see themselves as "people in recovery." Recovery mutual aid groups that once existed as closed systems in competition and conflict with one another are much more likely today to see themselves as part of a larger linked network of communities of recovery. Even co-attendance across religious, spiritual, and secular pathways of recovery is becoming common.

We are seeing on the heels of these trends the beginning cultural and political mobilization of people in recovery into a worldwide recovery advocacy movement whose core tenets include the following: 1) long-term addiction recovery is a reality in the lives of millions of individuals and families, 2) there are multiple pathways of long-term recovery, and 3) all pathways of recovery are cause for mutual celebration.

Contributions like *The Little Book* that chart the growing varieties of 12-Step experience and how the Steps are interpreted will only speed growth of this movement.

William L. White
Author, *Slaying the Dragon: The History of Addiction Treatment and Recovery in America*

Introduction

There are many versions of the 12-Step program of recovery. In fact, there are about as many versions as there are alcoholics in AA who use the program to get sober and to maintain their sobriety.

As a result, whole books have been devoted to analyzing and interpreting the 12 Steps in a way that reflects this variety. These include works, for example, such as Stephanie Covington's *A Woman's Way through the Twelve Steps* and Thérèse Jacobs-Stewart's book *Mindfulness and the 12 Steps*.

In Part One of this "Little Book," we are happy to present twenty alternative versions of the Steps, used and written by both individuals and groups.

Many years ago (1957), the co-founder of AA, Bill W., wrote:

> *We must remember that AA's Steps are suggestions only. A belief in them as they stand is not at all a requirement for membership among us. This liberty has made AA available to thousands who never would have tried at all, had we insisted on the Twelve Steps just as written.* (Alcoholics Anonymous Comes of Age, *p. 81)*

Consistent with the principles articulated by Bill W., agnostic and atheist individuals and groups in Alcoholics Anonymous often create their own alternative 12 Steps, replacing religious words like "God," "Him" and "Power" (all capitalized in the original Steps) with secular alternatives.

In Part Two of *The Little Book*, we present four brief interpretations of the Steps.

With these four interpretations, we are demonstrating the usefulness and value of Step interpretations. Reading them, you shall become well aware of the inevitability of interpreting the Steps.

In both parts of the book – "Alternatives" and "Interpretations" – we have left room for the readers to include their own version and interpretation of the Steps.

And then *The Little Book* concludes with Part Three. First, we have reproduced the original 12 Steps just as they were published in 1939.

Second, there is an article on the historical sources and people involved in the development of these original Steps called "The Origins of the Twelve Steps."

The 12 Steps – adapted as need be – can be an important tool in the process of recovery from alcoholism or addiction. You will no doubt like some of the alternatives and interpretations in this *Little Book* more than others. This just confirms our point: interpretation is an inescapable, useful and helpful part of working the Steps.

Part One:
Alternative 12 Steps

Twenty Versions

My Twelve Steps

Gabe's 12 Steps

1. We admitted we could not control our drinking, nor do without it, that our lives had become unmanageable.

2. We came to believe that others who had had or understood our problem could help us return to and maintain sanity.

3. We decided to accept what they said and act on their suggestions.

4. We made a searching inventory of our bad feelings, of those aspects of our own character that had contributed to these and of the harms we had done. We noted occasions where we had done well and were glad of these.

5. We showed the inventory to at least one other person and discussed it with them.

6. We accepted our moral and personal weaknesses, and accepted that they needed to change.

7. We became willing to admit those weaknesses to others, where appropriate, and to heed any advice that they might offer.

8. We became willing to make amends to those we had harmed.

9. We made direct amends to such people wherever possible, except when to do so would injure them or others.

10. We continued to take personal inventory, when we were wrong promptly admitted it and when we had done well, recognized this.

11. We adopted a practice of meditation and one of reflection upon our place in the world and how we could contribute to it.

12. Having experienced a psychic change as the result of these steps, we tried to carry this message to other alcoholics, and to practice these principles in all our affairs.

Inspired by his therapist, Gabe S. created this version of the 12 Steps. Gabe's version is perhaps typical of a secular alcoholic in recovery.

Beyond Belief Agnostics and Freethinkers

1. We admitted we were powerless over alcohol – that our lives had become unmanageable.

2. Came to accept and to understand that we needed strengths beyond our awareness and resources to restore us to sanity.

3. Made a decision to turn our will and our lives over to the care of the A.A. program.

4. Made a searching and fearless moral inventory of ourselves.

5. Admitted to ourselves without reservation, and to another human being, the exact nature of our wrongs.

6. Were ready to accept help in letting go of all our defects of character.

7. Humbly sought to have our shortcomings removed.

8. Made a list of all persons we had harmed and became willing to make amends to them all.

9. Made direct amends to such people wherever possible, except when to do so would injure them or others.

10. Continued to take personal inventory, and when we were wrong promptly admitted it.

11. Sought through mindful inquiry and meditation to improve our spiritual awareness, seeking only for knowledge of our rightful path in life and the power to carry that out.

12. Having had a spiritual awakening as the result of these steps, we tried to carry this message to alcoholics, and to practice these principles in all our affairs.

Beyond Belief Agnostics and Freethinkers was launched in Toronto on September 24, 2009. It's Canada's oldest active secular AA group.

Agnostic AA 12 Steps

1. We admitted we were powerless over alcohol - that our lives had become unmanageable.

2. Came to believe and to accept that we needed strengths beyond our awareness and resources to restore us to sanity.

3. Made a decision to entrust our will and our lives to the care of the collective wisdom and resources of those who have searched before us.

4. Made a searching and fearless moral inventory of ourselves.

5. Admitted to ourselves without reservation, and to another human being the exact nature of our wrongs.

6. Were ready to accept help in letting go of all our defects of character.

7. With humility and openness sought to eliminate our shortcomings.

8. Made a list of all persons we had harmed, and became willing to make amends to them all.

9. Made direct amends to such people wherever possible, except when to do so would injure them or others.

10. Continued to take personal inventory and when we were wrong, promptly admitted it.

11. Sought through meditation to improve our spiritual awareness and our understanding of the AA way of life and to discover the power to carry out that way of life.

12. Having had a spiritual awakening as a result of these steps, we tried to carry this message to alcoholics, and to practice these principles in all our affairs.

This version can be found on the AA Agnostics of the San Francisco Bay Area website, which lists a number of area agnostic groups and their meeting times and locations.

We Agnostics – Cleveland

1. We admitted we were powerless over alcohol - that attempts to control our drinking were futile and that our lives had become unmanageable.

2. Came to believe that even though we could not fix our problem by ourselves, circumstances and forces beyond our personal control could help restore us to sanity and balance.

3. Made a decision to accept things that were outside our control, especially what already is and to do the best with it.

4. Made a searching examination and a fearless inventory of ourselves.

5. Admitted to ourselves with total openness and to another human being, the exact nature of our wrongs.

6. Became willing to let go of our behaviors and personality traits that could be construed as defects and were creating problems.

7. With humility we acknowledged that we had these shortcomings and with openness we sought to eliminate these shortcomings.

8. Made a list of all persons we had harmed, and became willing to make amends to them all.

9. Made direct amends to such people wherever possible, except when to do so would injure them or others.

10. Continued to take personal inventory and when we were wrong promptly admitted it.

11. Sought through contemplation and meditation to improve self-awareness and adopted a spiritual approach to life as our primary purpose.

12. Having had a profound change in consciousness as the result of these steps, we tried to carry this message to alcoholics, and to practice these principles in all our affairs.

This version can be found on the We Agnostics website. The site states that these Steps originated in Cleveland and describes them as "training wheels" for the recovering alcoholic seeking his or her own spirituality.

Les Libres-penseurs, Saint-Hyacinthe (Quebec)

1. We admitted we were powerless over alcohol and our lives had become unmanageable.

2. We came to accept that we needed help to deal with our problem with alcohol.

3. We decided to join a group of people who had succeeded in putting an end to their drinking.

4. We calmly proceeded to a rigorous introspection of ourselves and recognized that our self-pity, our unfavorable behaviors and other adjustment disorders could have contributed to our alcoholism.

5. Without reservation, we recognized the importance of our introspection and shared the details of it with another person.

6. We have agreed to let go of our destructive behaviors towards ourselves and others.

7. We have sought, with humility, honesty and open-mindedness, to change our behaviors and our lifestyles in order to remain sober.

8. We made a list of all the people we had wronged and we chose to right our wrongs against each of them.

9. We have righted our wrongs directly against these people to the extent possible, except when to do so would harm them or others.

10. We continued our introspection and admitted our mistakes as soon as we realized them.

11. We searched within ourselves for our rightful place in life and the strength to realize ourselves there.

12. Having recovered by practicing these steps, we tried to share our experience with others and to apply the principles that underlie the steps in all areas of our lives.

This text, adapted from the steps which appear in the "Douze Traditions" (AA's French Publications Service, Montreal, 1986) was written by the AA group Les Libres-penseurs.

11.6.22
(ok, I like it.)

Humanist Twelve Steps

1. We accept the fact that all our efforts to stop drinking have failed.

2. We believe that we must turn elsewhere for help.

3. We turn to our fellow men and women, particularly those who have struggled with the same problem.

4. We have made a list of the situations in which we are most likely to drink.

5. We ask our friends to help us avoid those situations.

6. We are ready to accept the help they give us.

7. We honestly hope they will help.

8. We have made a list of the persons we have harmed and to whom we hope to make amends.

9. We shall do all we can to make amends, in any way that will not cause further harm.

10. We will continue to make such lists and revise them as needed.

11. We appreciate what our friends have done and are doing to help us.

12. We, in turn, are ready to help others who may come to us in the same way.

B.F. Skinner, the 1972 Humanist of the Year award winner, and a researcher and writer at Harvard University, drafted these Steps, which were first published in 1987.

The 12 Steps of Realistic Recovery

1. I can no longer deny I have an addiction, and admit my addiction can make me feel powerless, and that my choices and decisions while unaware or in denial of my addiction were destructive.

2. I came to believe that realistic and rational thinking could restore me from the insanity of addictive thinking.

3. I will let myself be helped by myself and others by using realistic and rational thinking and will never again turn my will and life over to addictive thinking.

4. I will make a realistic and rational evaluation or "inventory" of my thoughts, feelings and behaviours, both positive and negative. This is not to induce guilt and shame, but to evaluate where my attitudes, actions and decisions were not realistic or rational.

5. I will now admit to myself, the exact nature of my thoughts, feelings and behaviours, both positive and negative. I will share and review this evaluation with another willing person if I choose, unless where to do so would put myself or others at risk.

6. I am entirely ready to allow realistic and rational thinking to reveal my destructive patterns of addictive thinking and behaviour.

7. I will apply realistic and rational thinking and behaviour to replace my addictive thinking and behaviour.

8. I will make a list of all persons I have harmed, or been harmed by, in a way that might have enabled my addictive thinking.

9. I will take the responsibility of making amends and give the opportunity of receiving amends, except when to do so would put myself or others at risk.

10. I will continue to evaluate my life, and when my thoughts, feelings and behaviours are not realistic or rational, I will promptly admit it.

11. I will seek to improve my conscious awareness of reality, striving for the knowledge of what is real and rational and for the ability and determination to stop my addictive thinking and behaviour.

12. Having had progress towards a realistic and rational self-awareness away from addictive thinking as a result of what I have accomplished with these principles, I shall practice these principles in all areas of my life, and will be willing to share these principles with others who think they might gain from them.

Created by Mike H., January 2009, and found at his Realistic Recovery blog. Mike writes that he has chosen "to see Reality as a 'Higher Power,' since it was Reality I was trying to deny and escape from with my addictions."

→ what's reality?

SOS - 12 Statements

1. I have a life threatening problem. My past efforts to establish sobriety have been unsuccessful. I believe that I have choices and that my life no longer need be unmanageable. I accept responsibility for myself and my recovery.

2. I believe that a power within myself in tandem with supports and strengths beyond my own awareness and resources can restore me to a healthier, more balanced, and positive state of mind, body and soul.

3. I make a decision to entrust my will and life to the care of myself, the collective wisdom of those who have struggled with the same problem, and those in support of me.

4. I make a searching and fearless inventory of myself, of my strengths and weaknesses. I choose not to permit problems to overwhelm me, rather to focus on personal growth and the unconditional acceptance of others and myself.

5. I admit to myself, and if I choose, to another person or persons the exact nature of the negative, injurious aspects of my thinking and behavior. I explore the goodness within myself: the positive, courageous, and compassionate.

6. I focus on healing, abolishing self-blame and shame, and understanding the boundaries of my responsibilities. I remain open to the help and support of others as I address the challenge of change.

7. I embrace introspection and work towards alleviating my shortcomings. I strive for personal growth and fulfilment over perfection, and to become integrated with collective humanness.

8. I will consider those that I have harmed and those that have harmed me. I will become willing to explore my feelings regarding those harms.

9. I will make direct amends, as I deem appropriate and not injurious, to those whom I have harmed or negatively impacted and to myself.

10. I will continue sincere and meaningful self-evaluation, and strive for personal betterment.

11. I will seek to improve my awareness and understanding of myself, my addiction, and of other individuals and organizations with the common goal of arresting alcohol addiction.

12. With newfound acceptance and insight I will try to keep awareness, and compassion for others and myself, in the fore.

This list is found on the SOS (Secular Organization for Sobriety) website. SOS does not require or use steps, but an SOS individual can use whatever recovery tools he/she finds helpful.

The Alternative 12 Steps:
A Secular Guide to Recovery

1. Admit we are powerless over other people, random events and our own persistent negative behaviours, and that when we forget this, our lives become unmanageable.

2. Came to believe that spiritual resources can provide power for our restoration and healing.

3. Make a decision to be open to spiritual energy as we take deliberate action for change in our lives.

4. Search honestly and deeply within ourselves to know the exact nature of our actions, thoughts and emotions.

5. Will talk to another person about our exact nature.

6. Be entirely ready to acknowledge our abiding strength and release our personal shortcomings.

7. Work honestly, humbly and courageously to develop our assets and to release our personal shortcomings.

8. List all people we have harmed, including ourselves, and be willing to make amends to them all. Be willing to forgive those who have harmed us.

9. Whenever possible, we will carry out unconditional amends to those we have hurt, including ourselves, except when to do so would cause harm.

10. Continue to monitor ourselves, to acknowledge our successes and quickly correct our lapses and errors.

11. Increasingly engage spiritual energy and awareness to continue to grow in abiding strength and wisdom and in the enjoyment of life.

12. Practice the principles of these Steps in all our affairs and carry the 12-Step message to others.

Martha Cleveland, a psychologist, and Arlys G., a woman in recovery, wrote The Alternative 12 Steps: A Secular Guide to Recovery *in 1991. A second edition was published by AA Agnostica in 2014. The Steps are explained one chapter at a time in this pioneering book.*

White Bison

1. Honesty

2. Hope

3. Faith

4. Courage

5. Integrity

6. Willingness

7. Humility

8. Forgiveness

9. Justice

10. Perseverance

11. Spiritual Awakening

12. Service

White Bison uses the Medicine Wheel, a culturally appropriate recovery program for Native American people that has a single-word version of the Steps in which "each of the 12 Steps is presented from the perspective of the value that it reflects."

12 Secular Steps for Addiction Recovery

1. I admitted that I am an addict (alcoholic), and that my life had become unmanageable.

2. Came to believe that through honesty and effort, combined with the help of others, I could recover from addiction.

3. Made a decision to actively work a Twelve Step recovery plan to the best of my ability.

4. Completed a searching and fearless moral inventory of myself.

5. Honestly admitted to myself and to another human being the results of my inventory, including my defects of character.

6. Became willing to change defects in my character.

7. Accepted responsibility for my actions.

8. Listed all persons I had harmed, and became willing to make amends to them all.

9. Made direct amends to such people wherever possible, except when to do so would injure them or others.

10. Continued to take personal inventory, and when I was wrong, promptly admitted it.

11. Sought to improve my conscious awareness of ethical principles and values, and to use them consistently as standards for my decisions and actions.

12. Having matured as a person as a result of these Steps, I acknowledge my commitment to help others and to continue to use these principles in my daily life.

These are steps from the book Twelve Secular Steps: An Addiction Recovery Guide, *written by (another) Bill W. and published in 2018.*

A Buddhist's Non-Theist 12 Steps

1. We admitted our addictive craving over alcohol, and recognized its consequences in our lives.

2. Came to believe that a power other than self could restore us to wholeness.

3. Made a decision to go for refuge to this other power as we understood it.

4. Made a searching and fearless moral inventory of ourselves.

5. Admitted to ourselves and another human being the exact moral nature of our past.

6. Became entirely ready to work at transforming ourselves.

7. With the assistance of others and our own firm resolve, we transformed unskillful aspects of ourselves and cultivated positive ones.

8. Made a list of all persons we had harmed.

9. Made direct amends to such people where possible, except when to do so would injure them or others. In addition, made a conscientious effort to forgive all those who harmed us.

10. Continue to maintain awareness of our actions and motives, and when we acted unskillfully promptly admitted it.

11. Engaged through the practice of meditation to improve our conscious contact with our true selves, and seeking that beyond self. Also used prayer as a means to cultivate positive attitudes and states of mind.

12. Having gained spiritual insight as a result of these steps, we practice these principles in all areas of our lives, and make this message available to others in need of recovery.

These Steps were created by Bodhi, from Sydney, Australia. They were posted on Mike H.'s Realistic Recovery website. Bodhi writes that "Buddhism does not teach the doctrine of theism, but rather points out ways to live an enlightened, spiritual life without necessarily believing in God."

Buddhist 12 Steps

1. We admitted that we were powerless over our craving and addiction and that our lives have become unmanageable.

2. We came to believe that a Power greater than our individual selves could restore us to wholeness.

3. We made a decision to take refuge in and entrust ourselves to the compassion and guidance of a Greater Power of our understanding.

4. We made a searching and fearless moral inventory of our thoughts, words, and deeds.

5. We admitted to ourselves, our Greater Power, and another human being the precise moral nature of our thoughts, words, and deeds.

6. We became entirely ready to have our Greater Power transform our unwholesome characteristics into wholesome ones.

7. We humbly turned our unwholesome and unskilful qualities over to our Greater Power to be transformed into positive ones.

8. We made a list of all persons we had harmed, and became willing to make amends to them all.

9. We made direct amends to such people wherever possible, except when to do so would injure them or others.

10. We continued to remain mindful of our mental, verbal, and physical actions, and when we acted unskilfully, promptly admitted it.

11. We engaged in meditation and prayer in order to improve our conscious contact with our Greater Power (of our understanding) and to gain the insight and strength to realize and attain our Greater Power's compassionate aspiration for us.

12. Having realized a spiritual awakening as a result of these steps, we carry this message to others in need of recovery, and try to practice these principles in all our affairs.

Doug C.'s "A Buddhist's Insight into the 12 Steps of Recovery" was originally posted on the Buddhist Recovery Network. The network supports the use of Buddhist teachings, traditions and practices, in particular mindfulness and meditation, to help people recover from the suffering caused by addictive behaviours.

Islamic Twelve Steps to Recovery

1. We admitted that we were neglectful of our higher selves and that our lives have become unmanageable.

2. We came to believe that Allah could and would restore us to sanity.

3. We made a decision to submit our will to the will of Allah.

4. We made a searching and fearless moral inventory of ourselves.

5. We admitted to Allah and to ourselves the exact nature of our wrongs.

6. Asking Allah for right guidance, we became willing and open for change, ready to have Allah remove our defects of character.

7. We humbly ask Allah to remove our shortcomings.

8. We made a list of persons we have harmed and became willing to make amends to them all.

9. We made direct amends to such people wherever possible, except when to do so would injure them or others.

10. We continued to take personal inventory and when we were wrong promptly admitted it.

11. We sought through Salaat (prayer service) and Iqraa (reading and studying) to improve our understanding of Taqwa (G-d consciousness; proper Love and respect for Allah) and Ihsan (though we cannot see Allah, he can see us).

12. Having increased our level of Iman (faith) and Taqwa, as a result of applying these steps, we carried this message to humanity and began practicing these principles in all our affairs.

There are some 21 Millati Islami groups across the United States who use this adaptation of the Steps. Founded in Baltimore in 1989, the organization tries to "incorporate the Islamic Way of Life with the traditional Twelve Step approach."

Native American 12 Steps

1. We admitted we were powerless over alcohol, that we had lost control of our lives.

2. We came to believe that a power greater than ourselves could help us regain control.

3. We made a decision to ask for help from a Higher Power and others who understand.

4. We stopped and thought about our strengths and our weaknesses and thought about ourselves.

5. We admitted to the Great Spirit, to ourselves and to another person the things we thought were wrong about ourselves.

6. We are ready, with the help of the Great Spirit, to change.

7. We humbly ask a Higher Power and our friends to help us change.

8. We made a list of people who were hurt by our drinking, and want to make up for these hurts.

9. We are making up to those people whenever we can, except when to do so would hurt them more.

10. We continue to think about our strengths and weaknesses, and when we are wrong we say we are wrong.

11. We pray and think about ourselves, praying only for strength to do what is right.

12. We try to help other alcoholics and to practice these principles in everything we do.

This version was prepared for Native Americans by the Umatilla Tribal Alcohol Program and can be found on the Young Warriors Network, a site run by a group dedicated to providing healing services to First Nations and Métis peoples in Canada.

Neil's Twelve Steps

1. We admitted that we suffer from a seemingly hopeless state of mind and body.

2. Came to believe that we could recover.

3. Became open to changes in how we approach and respond to life.

4. Made a searching and fearless inventory of ourselves.

5. Reviewed our inventory with another human being.

6. Became entirely open to change.

7. Humbly affirmed our desire to change.

8. Made a list of all persons we had harmed and became ready to make amends to them all.

9. Made direct amends to such people wherever possible.

10. Continued to take personal inventory and when we were wrong promptly admitted it.

11. Sought through meditation to improve our understanding of ourselves, our program and our progress.

12. Having changed as the result of these steps, we tried to carry this message to alcoholics, and to practice these principals in all our affairs.

Neil F. describes these Steps as "my personal process. It is what I have used to guide my recovery and day to day living." He encourages others to use it or to create their own "from the original template so that you have a process that you are comfortable with and that works for you."

Gabe's Therapist's Version

1. Alcohol was something we could not do with, or without. Our lives and relationships were shattered.

2. We gained hope by talking to others who either have had or understood our problem.

3. We decided to accept what they said and act on their suggestions.

4. We needed to own our behaviour both good and bad.

5. We discussed it with someone else.

6. We identified those personal characteristics which had shaped our lives and accepted that they needed to change.

7. We asked for practical help in effecting these changes.

8. We made a list of those people whose lives had been affected adversely by our actions and behaviour, became prepared to make amends.

9. We repaired the harm we had done to them, whenever possible without doing further harm to ourselves or anyone else.

10. We continued to own our behaviour on a daily basis.

11. We tried to discover our own place in the world and to get in touch with our own personalities.

12. We became prepared to help others follow the same path.

Gabe S. was inspired by his therapist's 12 Steps. These Steps take a psychological approach to the program of recovery from alcoholism, an approach that has been common since the first days of AA.

The Twelve Steps of Self-Confirmation

1. I realize I am not in control of my use.

2. I acknowledge that a spiritual awakening can help me to find a new direction.

3. I am ready to follow and stay true to the new path I have chosen.

4. I have the strength and courage to look within and to face whatever obstacles hinder my continued personal and spiritual development.

5. I commit to become fully aware of how my use hurt those around me.

6. I am changing my life and developing my human potential.

7. I am proud of my strength and ability to grow.

8. I will do all I can to make up for the ways I have hurt myself and others.

9. I will take direct action to help others in any way that I can.

10. I will strive to be self-aware and follow the new path I have chosen.

11. I will continue to develop my potential through helping others and strive to become fully conscious of myself and life around me.

12. I will continue to develop my own human potential and spirituality and will actively help others who cannot control their use of alcohol.

These alternative 12 Steps are taken from Alcoholics Anonymous *and* The Counseling Profession: Philosophies in Conflict, *an article by Christine Le, Erik P. Ingvarson, and Richard C. Page. It was first published in the July/August 1995 issue of The Journal of Counseling & Development.*

Océane's 12 Steps

1. I understood that I would never stop drinking and live a normal life.

2. I thought to myself that maybe it was worth leaving the solution of my problem to someone who had already done so.

3. I decided to follow the advice of those in recovery.

4. Serenely, I honestly took stock of the pluses and minuses in my past life.

5. I shared this record with another human being.

6. It became clear that I had to change to lead a normal, alcohol-free life.

7. I sought help from my alcoholic friends as well as from competent professionals, especially in drug addiction.

8. I made a list of the people my alcoholism had hurt and looked for the reasons for my actions.

9. I apologized to those I hurt and, if possible, made up for them.

10. Every night I take stock of my day, promising myself to work on my most obvious shortcomings.

11. Through meditation, I connect to the Being within me and try to listen to my little inner voice; I trust this voice that I call my intuition.

12. By applying the steps, I experienced a spiritual awakening which leads me, on the one hand, to share my method with other alcoholics and, on the other hand, to apply my way of life in all areas of my life.

When she joined AA, Océane had never received any religious education. Her therapist, with whom she was looking for a solution to get out of her alcoholism, offered to write down the steps with her in her own way. The Océane steps are the result.

The Practical 12 Steps

1. Admitted we were caught in a self-destructive cycle and currently lacked the tools to stop it.

2. Trusted that a healthy lifestyle was attainable through social support and consistent self-improvement.

3. Committed to a lifestyle of recovery, focusing only on what we could control.

4. Made a comprehensive list of our resentments, fears and harmful actions.

5. Shared our lists with a trustworthy person.

6. Made a list of our unhealthy character traits.

7. Began cultivating healthy character traits through consistent positive behavior.

8. Determined the best way to make amends to those we had harmed.

9. Made direct amends to such people wherever possible, except when to do so would cause harm.

10. Practiced daily self reflection and continued making amends whenever necessary.

11. We started meditating.

12. Sought to retain our newfound recovery lifestyle by teaching it to those willing to learn and by surrounding ourselves with healthy people.

Jeffrey Munn is the author of Staying Sober Without God: The Practical 12 Steps to Long-Term Recovery From Alcoholism and Addictions. *It was published in January, 2019.*

My 12 Steps

1

2

3

4

5

6

7

8

9

10

11

12

Part Two:
Interpretations

Introduction

Four Interpretations of Each Step

Introduction

As we mentioned in the introduction to this book, there are at least as many interpretations of the Steps as there are alcoholics who "work" them.

To provide a sense of the scope of these interpretations of the Steps, we are highlighting the interpretations of four people.

The most important interpretation is that of the reader, especially if she or he is currently working the 12 Steps as a program of recovery. We have left room at the bottom of each Step for anyone who wishes to write down a personal interpretation of the Steps.

The first set of interpretations is by Dr. Allen Berger. An internationally recognized expert in the science of recovery, Dr. Berger wrote Hazelden's popular recovery mainstay, *12 Stupid Things That Mess Up Recovery* (2008);*12 Smart Things to Do When the Booze and Drugs Are Gone* (2010) and *12 Hidden Rewards of Making Amends* (2012). He is widely known for his work on several areas of recovery that include: integrating modern psychotherapy with the 12 Steps of Alcoholics Anonymous, emotional sobriety, helping new patients understand the benefits of group therapy, assisting families to adjust to the challenges of recovery, and training therapists and counsellors. His interpretations of the Steps come from his pamphlet "The Therapeutic Value of The 12 Steps."

The next author is Stephanie Covington. Her interpretations of the Steps are derived from her book, *A Woman's Way Through the Twelve Steps*. Dr. Covington is a pioneer in the field of women's issues, addiction, and recovery. She has developed an innovative, gender-responsive, and trauma-informed approach to the treatment needs of women. Her clients include the Betty Ford Treatment Center; the United Nations Office on Drugs and Crime; the Center for Substance Abuse Treatment in Washington, D.C.; the California Department of Corrections and Rehabilitation; and numerous other treatment and correctional settings. According to Linda R., whose review of Covington's book is on AA Agnostica, "the Steps are presented as tools to help alcoholics understand what their ultimate values are – their inner life – so that they can lead a life that is consistent with those values – their outer life – in their actions and relations with other people in the world around them." Written in 1994, *A Woman's Way* has become a favourite of many women in AA.

Next comes a set by Gabor Maté. Dr. Maté is a Hungarian-born Canadian physician who was for a time the staff physician at the Portland Hotel, a residence and resource centre for addicts in Vancouver's Downtown Eastside. He is the author of *In the Realm of Hungry Ghosts*. Maté derives the title from the Buddhist mandala, the Wheel of Life, which revolves through six realms, one of which is that of hungry ghosts. "This is the domain of addiction," he writes, "where we constantly seek something outside ourselves to curb an insatiable yearning for relief or fulfilment." Dr. Maté's interpretations are in Appendix IV of his book.

Dr. Maté writes at the beginning of the appendix:

> *Although I have not been an active participant in Twelve-Step programs, I see great value in the process they prescribe and recognize their effectiveness in helping many people to live in sobriety – or at least in abstinence. As explained in Chapter 32, abstinence is the avoidance of an addictive substance or behaviour. Sobriety is developing a mind-state focused not on staying away from something bad, but on living a life led by positive values and intentions. It means living in the present moment, neither driven by ghosts of the past nor lulled and tormented by fantasies and fears of the future.*

Finally, we have a set of interpretations by Thérèse Jacobs-Stewart. She is a practitioner of Buddhism, and her interpretations were culled from her book *Mindfulness and the 12 Steps*. Ms. Jacobs-Stewart is a counsellor, a founding member of a twelve-step and mindfulness group, and a woman in recovery. In 2004 she founded the Mind Roads Meditation Center, which is home to twelve steps and mindfulness meetings in St. Paul, Minnesota.

And then there is room put aside for you, the reader, to add your understanding of each of the Steps.

If you choose to fill in these parts, take your time.

Our views on the meaning of some of these Steps tend to evolve over time.

So we often need to return to them.

Indeed, some in recovery do them over and over again.

Four Interpretations of Each Step

	Step 1
	Step 1
Allen Berger	This Step helps us shatter our reliance on a false self, which was fed through lack of self-awareness, poor self-worth, and lack of language, plus denial, and a physical, mental and spiritual compulsion.
Stephanie Covington	The first step in recovery is to look inside ourselves. Turning inward is the beginning of becoming more truthful with ourselves. Honesty is essential because addictions thrive on dishonesty: we have become accustomed to hiding from our true feelings and values. (p. 15)
Gabor Maté	Step One accepts the full negative impact of the addiction process in one's life. It is a triumph over the human tendency to deny. We recognize that our resolution and strategies... have not liberated us ﾠ yup! from the addiction process and all its mechanisms that are deeply ingrained in our brains, emotions and behaviours.
Thérèse Jacobs-Stewart	By opening our hearts, admitting our powerlessness over alcohol, drugs, and other people's choices, we are able to remember we are part of the great stream of We. (p. 11)
	My Interpretation

Step 2	
Allen Berger	Hope is an important ingredient in all forms of healing. We are given hope, and humbled further because we won't be able to solve our problem on our own.
Stephanie Covington	What can we believe in? Whom can we trust? The problem is that life is more difficult and empty without someone or something to trust and believe in. (p. 27)
Gabor Maté	(A higher power) may, but does not necessarily, imply belief in a deity. It means heeding a higher truth than the immediate desires or terrors of the ego. (Dr. Maté provides a fuller understanding of the higher power concept in chapter 34 of his book *In the Realm of Hungry Ghosts*.)
Thérèse Jacobs-Stewart	We "come to" out of the fog of our deluded, addictive mind, reaching for something more. There, waiting for us, are the ancient practices of meditation and mindfulness. (p. 20)
My Interpretation	

Step 3	
Allen Berger	This Step is about commitment. We need to make a commitment to finding a new and more effective way of living.
Stephanie Covington	Of course, simple things aren't always easy. This Step says we turn our will over. When we cling to our will – our fierce determination that things should always go our way – we'll always be in conflict with something. Our wilfulness keeps us pushing against, not flowing with life. (p. 51)
Gabor Maté	The word God could have a religious meaning for many people. For many others, it means laying trust in the universal truths and higher values that reside at the spiritual core of human beings, but are feared and resisted by the grasping, anxious, past-conditioned ego.
Thérèse Jacobs-Stewart	We decide to let go of our delusions of control, and instead turn toward three specific spiritual practices. These practices are… taking refuge in awakening (buddha)… in the path of mindfulness, understanding, and love (dharma)… in community (sangha). (p. 30)
My Interpretation	

Step 4	
Allen Berger	The essence of this Step involves increasing our self-awareness, self-honesty, and insight into our behavior.
Stephanie Covington	When we carry intense guilt, we can hardly bear the thought of reviewing our past deeds. It may feel too painful to think about how we have hurt others and hurt ourselves. We may question the value of opening old wounds and remembering scenes we'd rather forget. It was a revelation to discover that Step Four wasn't just about agonizing about my past. Instead, it was about getting to know myself better. (p. 59)
Gabor Maté	The idea here is not self-condemnation, but the preparation of a clean slate for a life of sobriety. We search our conscience to identify where and how we have betrayed ourselves or others, not to wallow in guilt but to leave ourselves unburdened in the present and to help clear our path to the future.
Thérèse Jacobs-Stewart	In Step Four we are asked to look at parts of ourselves we are uncomfortable with, the parts that we reject and keep hidden out of fear or shame. (p. 49)
	My Interpretation

Step 5	
Allen Berger	We learn the value of self-disclosure, authenticity, and healthy relationships. This Step also continues to dismantle the false self and false pride and helps develop more humility and authenticity.
Stephanie Covington	The Fifth Step offers healing. It shows us how to create a new kind of relationship with people. We make ourselves vulnerable and open, allowing ourselves to be seen for who we really are, maybe for the first time. (p. 93)
Gabor Maté	Communicating the information – to ourselves in the form of a journal, or to some other human being – makes our moral self-searching into a concrete reality. Shame for ourselves is replaced by a sense of responsibility. We move from powerlessness to strength.
Thérèse Jacobs-Stewart	When we admit our wrongs and receive the acceptance and kind understanding of another human being in the Fifth Step, we begin the "healing into the depths" of our addictive mind. Taking Step Five can be the start of cultivating loving compassion towards ourselves. (p. 67)
My Interpretation	

Step 6

Allen Berger	We experience the pain of what we have done to hurt ourselves and others, and we begin to understand and develop insight into our behavioral patterns and the psychological functions of our character defects.
Stephanie Covington	In this Step we become willing to be open to change, willing to let go of habits or traits that cause our lives to be unbalanced. We become open to a deeper knowing and a clearer vision. (p. 95)
Gabor Maté	We accept that our missteps and our lack of integrity do not represent who we really are and commit to let go of these tendencies as they continue to arise in the future – for they surely will.
Thérèse Jacob-Stewart	The Eastern view is that defects of character are rooted in confusion, based on deluded ideas about ourselves and others. Mindfulness practice develops the clarity to cut through our confusion, getting to the root of it. Once we become aware of a delusion, its spell is broken. (p. 79)

My interpretation

Step 7	
Allen Berger	We are learning the importance of being vulnerable and asking for help. This is important in attaining more humility.
Stephanie Covington	But for all of our awareness, we may still not accept ourselves. Step Seven gives us the opportunity to move from self-awareness to self-acceptance. Acceptance is the key to change. Another paradox I have learned in recovery is that when I accept myself just as I am, I can change. (p. 120)
Gabor Maté	Our shortcomings are where we fall short of, and even lose sight of, our true potential Thus, in giving up the short-term rewards of addictive behaviours, we are choosing a vast enrichment of who we are. Humility is in order in place of pride, that desperate grandiosity of the ego.
Thérèse Jacobs-Stewart	We felt the pain of our defects in Step Six. We find it uncomfortable to be self-absorbed, or bitter, or filled with fear. We don't want to be separated from our true nature any longer; it's painful to veil it in delusion and choke its expression. (p. 100)
My interpretation	

	Step 8
Allen Berger	The lessons taught in this Step have to do with the fundamentals of healthy communication; delivering our message to the proper person and being as specific as possible.
Stephanie Covington	Where is there ongoing bitterness, animosity, fear or hostility in our relationships? Whom do we resent or avoid? But as we continue to work this Step, we realize that "harm" has other meanings as well. We might want to consider relationships that feel unresolved – whether we believe we've harmed someone or not. Is there unfinished business to attend to? (p. 122)
Gabor Maté	We are prepared to accept responsibility for each and every sin of commission or omission we have perpetrated on people in our lives.
Thérèse Jacobs-Stewart	Finding Pearls in the Dust-bin: Step Eight invites us to strip off the armor of our denial, to let go of rationalizing, justifying, or blaming others for our actions. (p.115)
My interpretation	

Step 9	
Allen Berger	We learn to be responsible for our behavior; we learn how to respect others; and we learn that we are as important as others, no more and no less.
Stephanie Covington	What does it mean to make amends to another person? It means taking responsibility for your part in a relationship. Responsibility refers to the ability to respond appropriately. When you do, you extend hope for something new to yourself and to another person. (p. 137)
Gabor Maté	Step Nine is not about us, but about others. Its purpose is not to make us feel or look good, but to provide restitution where that's appropriate... Our fears of how we will look to others should neither drive this step nor inhibit it.
Thérèse Jacobs-Stewart	Once we have atoned for our wrongs – even if the other person is not inclined to forgive us, even if this person is not willing to own his or her part in the difficulty – we need to let go... We can experience the relief of having no secrets, making no excuses, and holding no pretences. (p. 119)
My interpretation	

Step 10	
Allen Berger	This Step concerns maintaining our humility, being honest with ourselves, and guarding against false pride.
Stephanie Covington	Now we make a daily commitment to continuing observation and reflection – recognizing when we're out of balance or hurting ourselves or others. Our ongoing awareness allows us to meet each day and each relationship with responsibility. (p. 152)
Gabor Maté	This is Step Four in action. As human beings, most of us are far away from attaining perfect saintliness in all our behaviours or interactions, and therefore can afford to give up the process of moral self-inventory only when they lower us into the ground.
Thérèse Jacobs-Stewart	Ongoing mindfulness helps us notice the pressure in our chest, the hairs rising on our neck, or the toxic thoughts that precede an emotional hijack. Regular on-the-spot checks – before, during, or after our actions – help us have fewer emotional or relationship messes to clean up. (p. 131)
	My interpretation

Step 11	
Allen Berger	Maintenance is not enough. We need to continue to grow or we will regress. This Step is about expanding our consciousness and continuing to seek more knowledge about our new way of life.
Stephanie Covington	We can choose whatever practice gives us a sense of inner peace. (p. 173)
Gabor Maté	This is not a demand for submission but a suggested path to freedom. Human life, I believe, is balanced on four pillars: physical health, emotional integration, intellectual awareness and spiritual practice. There are no prescriptions for the latter.
Thérèse Jacobs-Stewart	In Step Eleven, we find that making conscious contact with Great Reality deep down within us provides a quiet peace, quenching, at last, our restless yearnings. (p. 143)
My interpretation	

Step 12	
Allen Berger	We develop a new purpose to our life that is not about us. We discover the importance of being of value to others, and we learn that we need to maintain our integrity in all our affairs.
Stephanie Covington	With recovery this can mean that we offer a straightforward explanation of the Twelve Steps, as well as our own personal experience – how we reworked, translated, revised, or otherwise molded the Steps until they were relevant to us. We all have more to offer than the party line and a by-the-book recitation of the Steps. We can share our story any way we like. (p. 188)
Gabor Maté	Carrying the message to others means manifesting the principles of integrity, truth, sobriety and compassion in our lives. It may call for providing support and leadership when appropriate and welcome, but does not mean proselytizing on behalf of any program, group or set of beliefs.
Thérèse Jacobs-Stewart	Through the Twelve Step program, we cross over to a new way of living. We awaken to freedom from cravings, shallow desires, and clinging to what we cannot change… We can live the way of kindness in the world, in "all our affairs," and let our true face shine. (p. 164)
My interpretation	

Part Three:
History

The Original 12 Steps

The Origins of the 12 Steps

AA Agnostica

The Original 12 Steps

1. We admitted we were powerless over alcohol – that our lives had become unmanageable.

2. Came to believe that a Power greater than ourselves could restore us to sanity.

3. Made a decision to turn our will and our lives over to the care of God as we understood Him.

4. Made a searching and fearless moral inventory of ourselves.

5. Admitted to God, to ourselves, and to another human being the exact nature of our wrongs.

6. Were entirely ready to have God remove all these defects of character.

7. Humbly asked Him to remove our shortcomings.

8. Made a list of all persons we had harmed and became willing to make amends to them all.

9. Made direct amends to such people wherever possible, except when to do so would injure them or others.

10. Continued to take personal inventory, and when we were wrong promptly admitted it.

11. Sought through prayer and meditation to improve our conscious contact with God as we understood Him, praying only for knowledge of His will for us and the power to carry that out.

12. Having had a spiritual awakening as the result of these steps, we tried to carry this message to alcoholics and to practice these principles in all our affairs.

Copyright © Alcoholics Anonymous World Services, Inc.

The original 12 Steps were written by the co-founder of Alcoholics Anonymous, Bill W., and published in 1939.

The Origins of the 12 Steps

One alcoholic talking to another (Step 12)

It all began in the waning months of 1934.

Bill W., an incorrigible inebriate nearing the end of his rope, was visited at his home by Ebby T., a former schoolmate and friend. Ebby was no stranger to alcohol and had done time in jail and mental hospitals to prove it.

Bill expected to spend the day drinking and reliving old times with his friend, but Ebby would have none of it. He had found sobriety and wanted instead to share his "experience, strength and hope" with Bill. "On a chill November afternoon in 1934 it was Ebby who had brought me the message that saved my life," Bill would later say in his eulogy to his old friend.

But that salvation was not quite immediate. Waving a bottle of beer, Bill staggered up the steps of the Towns Hospital for Alcohol and Drug Addiction for his fourth and last time on the afternoon of December 11, 1934. Ebby visited him there on December 14 and once again carried his message of sobriety to his friend. Bill never drank again after Towns Hospital and understood that the experience of "one alcoholic talking to another" had been the key to his sobriety.

Indeed, four months later Bill would carry the message to another alcoholic. On a business trip to Akron, Ohio, afraid he might relapse, Bill arranged a meeting with Dr. Bob S. It certainly was an experience of one alcoholic talking to another: Dr. Bob had insisted the meeting be limited to 15 minutes but was so moved by Bill's understanding and the fact that he shared from his own personal experience that the discussion lasted six hours.

Bill stayed at Dr. Bob's home working with him from May 12 to June 10, 1935, when Dr. Bob took his last drink.

Bill and Dr. Bob, of course, are recognized as the co-founders of Alcoholics Anonymous. And June 10, 1935, is generally considered the founding date of AA – an acknowledgment that "in the kinship of common suffering, one alcoholic talking to another" would forever be the fundamental principle of the fellowship of AA.

This principle is given prominence as the last step of the 12 Steps. "Carrying the message" in AA is the foundation of a life of sobriety. AA meetings are most often organized around a speaker or a discussion where alcoholics are provided with an opportunity to share with each other. There are no lectures in AA; the need for them is obviated by the "sharing circle" and the insights derived therefrom. The centrality of this principle was understood and acknowledged by all in early AA, well before the fellowship was called "AA" and before the "Big Book," *Alcoholics Anonymous*, was published.

Transformation (The Middle Steps)

The difference between an alcoholic who needs help and an alcoholic who might be able to provide it is transformation.

Recovery from alcoholism is more often than not about change. That change involves a shift in the way the alcoholic understands the world around her or him as well as how the other people in that world are understood and treated.

Steps 2 through 11 are meant to be the means to bring about that change.

Most 12-Steppers would agree with the above. However, how this transformation is understood varies from one person to the next.

In AA, there were from the very beginning two different ways of understanding this transformation; one of them was religious and the other psychological.

The Oxford Group

The religious interpretation comes from the Oxford Group, a Christian evangelical movement that had its heyday in the 1930s.

Ebby T. had been bailed out, literally, by members of an Oxford Group. Facing incarceration in a mental institution for public drunkenness, Ebby was placed in the care of three members of an Oxford Group and was then residing at the Group's base in the Calvary Rescue Mission in New York, not too far from where Bill lived.

It was the Oxford Group message that Ebby brought to Bill in 1934. Bill would later report that "early AA got its ideas of self-examination, acknowledgment of character defects, restitution for harm done, and working with others straight from the Oxford Groups." (*Alcoholics Anonymous Comes of Age*, p. 39)

And God. The idea of God comes from the Oxford Group.

In the Steps as they were published in 1939, half of the Steps contain a reference to God. The first is a reference to "a Power greater than ourselves"

(Step 2), two refer to "God, as we understood Him" (Steps 3 and 11), another two simply say "God" (Steps 5 and 6) and one refers to God as "Him" (Step 7).

That's a lot of God for a few short sentences.

Moreover, this is a specific, theistic conception of God. Theism conceives of God as personal and active in the governance of the world. In the Steps, one can have "conscious contact with God" (Step 11) and God can do things such as remove our defects of character and our shortcomings (Steps 6 and 7). This interventionist God (the "Big Book" says that "God could and would if He were sought"), derived from the Oxford Group, is a Christian conception of God.

Many of the Steps also recommend behaviours that have historically been part of religious practice. These include self-surrender (Step 3: "Made a decision to turn our will and our lives over to the care of God"), confession of sins (Step 5: "Admitted to God, to ourselves, and to another human being"), atonement or restitution (Steps 8 and 9: "Made a list... (and) made direct amends... wherever possible"), and spreading the gospel (Step 12: "we tried to carry this message").

"The substantive faith set forth in especially the first three Steps of *Alcoholics Anonymous*," Ernest Kurtz wrote in his classic and authoritative work on the history of AA, "was in salvation attained through a conversion, the pre-condition of which was the act of surrender." (*Not-God: A History of Alcoholics Anonymous*, p. 182)

The relationship between the Oxford Group and AA is described in Chapter VIII ("The Context of the History of Religious Ideas") of Kurtz's book, a must-read for those interested in the religiosity of AA.

He describes the "Evangelical Pietism" of the Oxforders. The "evangelical" part involves a fervour for carrying the message of the gift of an omnipotent God. The "pietism" part expresses an aversion to the idea that humans are sufficient unto themselves. These ideas blossomed in the mid-1930s, were present in the Oxford Group, and influenced a nascent AA.

From an Oxfordian point of view, real sobriety - not one of the "dry drunk" variety - was in essence salvation, the result of a religious conversion.

Rowland H. was one of the Oxford Groupers who had rescued Ebby from being committed to a mental institution. Rowland had been told by Carl Jung that he was an incurable alcoholic. The only thing that could save him was conversion; alcoholics of his kind could only be saved by vital spiritual experiences: "huge emotional displacements and rearrangements. Ideas, emotions and attitudes which were once the guiding forces of the lives of these men are suddenly cast to one side, and a completely new set of conceptions and motives begin to dominate them." (*Alcoholics Anonymous*, p. 27)

A few days after Ebby visited him at his home, Bill showed up in a drunken state at the Calvary Rescue Mission in search of his friend. It was his first Oxford Group meeting. "Something touched me. I guess it was more than that. I was hit." Not long afterward he was at the Towns Hospital, where he had his own "white light" conversion experience, the kind of vital spiritual experience that Jung had described to Rowland H. "After that experience, he never again doubted the existence of God." (*Pass It On*, p. 121) Coming out of the Towns Hospital, Bill was a committed member of the Oxford Groups.

Listening to audio tapes of Bill W. today, it often seems that when he talks about God, what he is saying more than anything else is that he, Bill, is not in charge, that it's not him deciding to take one breath after another, it's not him deciding that his heart will beat or continue to beat, or won't. In a sense, when Bill talks about the "grace of God" what he seems to be suggesting is that there is a certain gratuitousness to existence and we ought to be thankful for it, while acknowledging we are not in control.

Still, the word "God" (or "Power" or "Him") appears six times in the Steps, and the practices described have historically been designed to win redemption, that is, to satisfy the demands of a judgmental and interventionist deity. That they might also help to allay the cravings of an incorrigible alcoholic seems something of an accident, an idea that falls into the category of an afterthought.

The Steps, as inherited from the Oxford Group, are religious. To suggest otherwise demonstrates a poor understanding of history and of the facts and is disingenuous at best.

This is certainly the opinion of the high courts in the United States. They have repeatedly reviewed the evidence at hand and concluded that "a fair reading of the fundamental A.A. doctrinal writings discloses that their dominant theme is unequivocally religious." (New York Court of Appeals, 1996)

But does that mean an alcoholic has to "get religion" to use the 12 Steps to bring about a transformation that will nurture and protect a life of sobriety?

Not on your life.

Agnostics and Atheists

From Bill's earliest attempts to articulate – and enumerate – a path of recovery from alcoholism, there have been many restatements and qualifications of the Steps, and of their meaning and intent.

Between the first printing of the first edition of *Alcoholics Anonymous: The Story of How More Than One Hundred Men Have Recovered From Alcoholism* (the original title of the book) in April 1939, and the second printing two years later in March 1941, it became evident that a restatement of the principles of the AA program of recovery was essential. That objective was achieved with the addition of Appendix II: Spiritual Experience.

The appendix clarifies the nature of the transformation necessary for recovery from alcoholism: "Though it was not our intention to create such an impression, many alcoholics have nevertheless concluded that in order to recover they must acquire an immediate and overwhelming 'God-consciousness' followed at once by a vast change in feeling and outlook." The correction comes next: "Most of our experiences are what the psychologist William James calls the 'educational variety' because they develop slowly over a period of time."

Let's skip back a few years: Before Bill left Towns Hospital for the last time, Ebby brought him a copy of William James' book, *The Varieties of Religious Experience*. For James, religious experience was valuable because of what it said about our human nature and psychology. James was very popular among the earliest AAers, in large part because his Varieties was in many ways the bridge between those who viewed the changes necessary for recovery as religious and those who saw them as purely psychological, or "spiritual," if you will, certainly devoid of religious creed or affiliation.

The appendix makes this link as well; spiritual experience or awakening is equated with a personality change. This change need be neither sudden nor religious, nor does it of necessity involve a God.

In sum, and in line with a purely psychological understanding, the salvation of an alcoholic depends upon a "personality change sufficient to bring about recovery from alcoholism."

Anybody can work with that.

Let's back up a bit now to the early days of AA...

In the first few years of AA, before this appendix was added and before the publication and printing of the 12 steps, the fellowship – then one group in each of New York, Akron, and Cleveland - shared a "word-of-mouth" recovery program.

As Bill put it ("Where Did The Twelve Steps Come From", AA Grapevine, 1953):

> *As we commenced to form a society separate from the Oxford Group, we began to state our principles something like this:*
>
> 1.   *We admitted that we were powerless over alcohol.*
> 2.   *We got honest with ourselves.*
> 3.   *We got honest with another person, in confidence.*
> 4.   *We made amends for harms done others.*
> 5.   *We worked with other alcoholics without demand for prestige or money.*
> 6.   *We prayed to God to help us to do these things as best we could.*
>
> *This was the gist of our message to incoming alcoholics up to 1939, when our present Twelve Steps were put to paper.*

Six steps! And this word-of-mouth program is more secular than religious – "God" is mentioned only in the last step.

Looking back, these "Steps" must have worked well for those men then in the fellowship. Those with a religious inclination had their God in the last step. And the radical atheists and agnostics and the liberals in the middle would have had a perfectly workable psychological program of recovery. Moreover, "these principles were advocated according to the whim or liking of each of us," Bill added.

So why mess with perfection and draft a new 12-Step program?

The fellowship was working on the book that would come to be called *Alcoholics Anonymous* (although at the time the more popular title was *The Way Out*), and they had arrived at Chapter Five, which would be named "How it Works," and would include the program of recovery.

Bill remembers: "I split the word-of-mouth program up into smaller pieces… I was surprised that in a short time, perhaps half an hour, I had set down certain principles which, on being counted, turned out to be twelve in number." So that's where the 12 Steps come from. Bill continues, "For some unaccountable reason, I had moved the idea of God into the Second Step, right up front. Besides I had named God very liberally throughout the other steps. In one of the steps I had even suggested that the newcomer get down on his knees."

Just goes to show: the Steps you end up with depend upon the guy or gal who sits down to write them.

The result was predictable and well-deserved.

> *When the document was shown to our New York meeting the protests were many and loud. Our agnostic friends didn't go at all for the idea of kneeling. Others said we were talking all too much about God. And anyhow, why should there be twelve steps when we had done fine on six? Let's keep it simple, they said. This sort of heated discussion went on for days and nights.*

Eventually, a compromise was reached. Kneeling was removed from Step 7. In Step 2, "God" was changed to "a Power greater than ourselves." In Steps 3 and 11, and directly attributed to the agnostics Hank P. and Jim B., "God" was changed to "God as we understood Him." Finally, and this was perhaps the clincher, "As a lead-in sentence to all the steps we wrote these words: 'Here are the steps we took which are suggested as a Program of Recovery.' AA's Twelve Steps were to be suggestions only." (Alcoholics AACA, p. 167)

Bill called the compromise a "ten-strike," which presumably has something to do with bowling, and added:

> *Such were the final concessions to those of little or no faith; this was the great contribution of our atheists and agnostics. They had widened our gateway so that all who suffer might pass through, regardless of their belief or lack of belief.*

In hindsight, it was certainly not a "ten-strike." The ball didn't end up in the gutter, but it turned out to be more of a "split," with pins on both sides and far apart, rather than a "ten-strike."

God as we understood Him. Certainly the expressions "God as we understood Him" and "a Power greater than ourselves" are an invitation to interpret the meaning of the Steps. In fact, interpretation is not an option, but a matter of necessity.

For the non-believer, this power or God is generally understood as the internal or external resource or resources accessed and relied upon to get sober and maintain sobriety.

Along these lines, a cultural anthropologist – not even discussing the 12 Steps of AA - once observed:

> *We always rely on something that transcends us, some system of ideas and powers in which we are embedded and which support us. This power is not always obvious. It need not be overtly a god...It can be the power of an all-absorbing activity, a passion, a dedication to a game, a way of life… (Ernest Becker,* The Denial of Death, *p. 55)*

This is a psychological understanding of a higher power writ large.

And so agnostic and atheist AAers have been known to talk about GOD as "Good Orderly Direction" or a "Group of Drunks."

That's arduous, though. It's awkward, to say the least, given the explicit religiosity of the Steps.

One can with rigorous honesty write a personal version of the Steps or share a group's alternative Steps. One agnostic version represents the "God" of Step 3 like this, for example: "Made a decision to entrust our will and our lives to the care of the collective wisdom and resources of those who have searched before us." That, or something very similar to that, has worked for many a recovering alcoholic in AA.

A suggested program of recovery. There are no requirements for membership in AA. The Steps are not mandatory. A person makes a personal choice to "work the Steps," or not.

And if a newcomer chooses to do the Steps and the God part is an obstacle to recovery, then it should be removed or replaced. As the author of the Steps said:

> *We must remember that AA's Steps are suggestions only. A belief in them as they stand is not at all a requirement for membership among us. This liberty has made AA available to thousands who never would have tried at all, had we insisted on the Twelve Steps just as written. (AACA, p. 81)*

AA is first and foremost a fellowship, "one alcoholic talking to another;" it is not a program. It has a program, a "suggested" program, and doesn't claim privileged insights into recovery from alcoholism.

The important thing in getting sober and maintaining sobriety is the "personality change sufficient to bring about recovery from alcoholism."

How that change is achieved varies from one person to the next.

Powerlessness over alcohol does not mean that an alcoholic is powerless over the decisions that are key to her or his recovery and life.

However, we're jumping ahead: "powerlessness" is the topic of the final section of this essay, a section devoted to the first of the twelve Steps.

Meanwhile, the agnostics and atheists in AA back in the late '30s and '40s got on with their lives, their lives in sobriety and in AA, after the publication of the 12 Steps. And they did it – of course – according to their own "whim and liking."

One of the better-known atheists of the day was Jim B. He is credited with the "as we understood Him" in both Steps 3 and 11 and with Tradition Three: "The only requirement for AA membership is a desire to stop drinking."

Jim presented quite a challenge to the group, as he later wrote in Sober for Thirty Years. "I started fighting nearly all the things Bill and the others stood for, especially religion, the 'God bit.' But I did want to stay sober, and I did love the understanding Fellowship."

At one point, his group held a prayer meeting to decide what to do with him. "The consensus seems to have been that they hoped I would either leave town or get drunk."

Over time, though, there was a change in Jim, a transformation. It could hardly be called a conversion. Soon he took a kinder attitude towards the other members of the Group who believed in a God. Perhaps their belief did help them stay sober, he mused. "Who am I to say?" And that became his new approach to those with views contrary to his own.

An exemplary, if not essential, attitude in the rooms of AA.

But that does not mean he "got religion." Jim B went on to start AA groups in Philadelphia, Baltimore and San Diego. As Clarence Snyder, a founder of the first AA group in Cleveland, reported: "Jimmy remained steadfast, throughout his life and 'preached' his particular brand of AA wherever he went." (*How it Worked: The Story of Clarence H. Snyder and the Early Days of Alcoholics Anonymous in Cleveland, Ohio*, p. 107)

Another agnostic member of the New York AA group was Ray W. On a business trip to San Francisco, he also planned to meet with some alcoholics to get them started in AA. Bill got him to bring the new book *Alcoholics Anonymous* with him and when he gave copies of it to the alcoholics, he told them: "Now boys, this AA is great stuff. It really saved my life. But there's one feature of it I don't like. I mean this God business. So when you read the book, you can skip that part of it." (AACA, p. 88)

Hitting Bottom (Step 1)

Before the first meeting, no one ever thinks it would be lovely to spend a lot evenings in the rooms of AA with a bunch of alcoholics.

But that's what a good number of women and men do.

The cause of this affinity for AA meetings is described as "hitting bottom." The alcoholic – often after years of denial – comes to the end of the rope, and this can be both a psychological and physical cul-de-sac from which there is only one way out: the rooms of AA.

This idea of hitting bottom was given credence in William James book, *The Varieties of Religious Experience*. Reading it in the Town's Hospital after it had been passed on to him by Ebby, Bill was especially struck by this: "In most of the cases described (in the book), those who had been transformed were hopeless people. In some controlling area of their lives they had met absolute defeat." (*The Language of the Heart*, p. 197)

Bill described this as "deflation at depth," a term he thought, erroneously, that he had gotten from James.

While at Towns Hospital, Bill was under the care of a rather remarkable physician, a specialist in addiction and the Medical Director of the hospital, Dr. William Silkworth.

Silkworth, watching Bill flounder in his efforts to help other alcoholics, urged him to emphasize "hitting bottom" and to talk about the medical and other catastrophes related to drinking, as a first step in helping other alcoholics to deal with their affliction.

> *Bill, you've got the cart before the horse. You've got to deflate these people first. So give them the medical business, and give it to them hard. Pour it right into them about the obsession that condemns them to drink and the physical sensitivity or allergy of the body that condemns them to go mad or die if they keep on drinking. Coming*

from an alcoholic, one alcoholic talking to another, maybe that will crack those tough egos deep down. (AACA, p. 68)

Silkworth was the first 20th century medical doctor to hold that alcoholism was a physical illness, rather than the result of some form of moral failure. In the thirties, shortly after the end of the temperance movement, this was a revolutionary idea. "Physically, a man has developed an illness," he wrote of the alcoholic. "He cannot use alcohol in moderation, at least not for a period of enduring length. If the alcoholic starts to drink, he sooner or later develops the phenomenon of craving."

This will sound eerily familiar to a person with some experience in the rooms of AA. It was the doctor's first publication and appeared on March 17, 1937, in the Medical Record under the title Alcoholism as a Manifestation of Allergy.

In arguing that it is the direct result of a physical and medical problem, Silkworth asserted that true alcoholism is "the result of gradually increasing sensitization by alcohol over a more or less extended period of time" until the condition is fully established.

Silkworth wrote that the alcoholic can go for years without a drink, but is yet not free: "a single drink will develop the full symptomatology again."

His opinion is rather well-summarized here: "The patient cannot use alcohol at all for physiological reasons. He must understand and accept the situation as a law of nature operating inexorably."

Dr. Silkworth also wrote The Doctor's Opinion in The "Big Book".

There it is then, Step 1: "We admitted that we were powerless over alcohol – that our lives had become unmanageable." It comes directly from William James and the Medical Director of the Towns Hospital, William Silkworth.

This piece on The Origins of the 12 Steps began at the Towns Hospital, and will now end back at the Towns Hospital.

Let us briefly summarize our findings. We have in AA a program of recovery based on the simple principle of one alcoholic talking to another. And we have steps - understood in a variety of ways - that can result in a personality change sufficient to bring about and support a life free from alcohol. That's if – and this was our final point – if the alcoholic remembers that alcoholism is a physical affliction that simply will not allow her or him to pick up that first drink.

We move on now from these beginnings, these origins. We go forward, one simple step at a time.

AA Agnostica

AA Agnostica is meant to be a helping hand for the alcoholic who reaches out to Alcoholics Anonymous for help and finds that she or he is disturbed by the religious content of many AA meetings.

AA Agnostica is not affiliated with any group in AA or any other organization.

Contributors to the AA Agnostica website are all members of Alcoholics Anonymous, unless otherwise indicated. The views they express are neither their groups' nor those of AA, but solely their own.

There is an increasing number of groups within AA that are not religious in their thinking or practice. These groups don't recite prayers at the beginning or ending of their meetings, nor do they suggest that a belief in God is required to get sober or to maintain sobriety. If the readings at their meetings include AA's suggested program of recovery, then a secular or humanist version of the 12 Steps is shared.

If you asked members of AA who belong to these non-religious groups about their vision of the fellowship, they would probably describe it this way:

> **ALCOHOLICS ANONYMOUS** is a fellowship of men and women who share their experience, strength and hope with each other that they may solve their common problem and help others recover from alcoholism. The only requirement for AA membership is a desire to stop drinking. There are no dues or fees for membership: we are self-supporting through our own contributions. AA is not allied with any sect, denomination, politics, organization or institution: neither endorses nor opposes any causes. Our primary purpose is to stay sober and help other alcoholics to achieve sobriety.

AA Agnostica does not endorse or oppose any form of religion or atheism. Our only wish is to ensure suffering alcoholics that they can find sobriety in AA without having to accept anyone else's beliefs or having to deny their own.

The word "Agnostica" is derived from Chapter Four, "We Agnostics," of *Alcoholics Anonymous*, otherwise known as the "Big Book". When we use the word "agnostic" in relation to AA – or words like "atheist" or "freethinker" – we are simply referring to the specific wisdom of groups and individuals within the fellowship who understand that a belief in "God" is not necessary for recovery from alcoholism.

(`SAA` agnostica?)

The experience, strength and hope of these women and men form the basis for the pages and posts on the AA Agnostica website and are often a comfort and an inspiration for others in AA.